Praise for

Make Someone Smile

"Forty very basic and very powerful ways for children to add peace to their lives. Even the pictures make you smile and feel that the next generation is on the way to a better world."—*American Booksellers*

"Best bet for a teacher's bookshelf. A wonderful read-aloud book that will prompt discussion about resolving conflict, being a friend, and using appropriate behavior. Charming and ideal for children of all ages."—*Schooldays*

Make Someone Smile

...and 40 More Ways to Be a Peaceful Person

Written by
Judy Lalli

Photographs by
Douglas L. Mason-Fry

free spirit
PUBLISHING®
Works for kids®

Library of Congress Cataloging-in-Publication Data
Lalli, Judy, 1949–
    Make someone smile : and 40 more ways to be a peaceful person / by Judy Lalli ; with photographs by Douglas L. Mason-Fry.
       p. cm.
    Summary: A collection of photographs of children modeling the skills of peacemaking and conflict resolution.
    ISBN 0-915793-99-7 (alk. paper)
    1. Peace—Pictorial works. 2. Peace—Juvenile literature. [1. Peace—Pictorial works.]
I. Mason-Fry, Douglas L., 1950– ill. II. Title.
JX1964.L38   1996
302.3'4—dc20
                  95-39198
                  CIP
                  AC

Author photograph by John Kellar Photography
Book design by MacLean & Tuminelly
Cover design by Marieka Heinlen

15 14 13 12 11 10 9 8 7
Printed in Canada

Free Spirit Publishing Inc.
217 Fifth Avenue North, Suite 200
Minneapolis, MN 55401-1299
(612) 338-2068
help4kids@freespirit.com
www.freespirit.com

The following are registered trademarks of Free Spirit Publishing Inc.:

FREE SPIRIT®
FREE SPIRIT PUBLISHING®
THE FREE SPIRITED CLASSROOM®
SELF-HELP FOR KIDS®
SELF-HELP FOR TEENS®
WORKS FOR KIDS®
HOW RUDE!™
LEARNING TO GET ALONG™
LAUGH & LEARN™

free spirit
PUBLISHING®
Works for kids®

Learning to Get Along™

Laugh & Learn™

Dedication

I treasure the support and encouragement of my friends.
This book is lovingly dedicated to them.

Acknowledgments

I would like to thank the children who inspired this book: Aaron, Alex, Anthony, Ashley, Chris, Denise, Fontella, Jee Sung, Katie, Marcus, Marques, Michele, Nicole, Ramone, Sarah, Shakeema, Tameisha, Tim C., Tim F., Tim O., and Vicky; their families, who allowed their pictures to appear; and the staff and students of Paul V. Fly School in Norristown, Pennsylvania, who contributed suggestions and gave enthusiastic support.

I would also like to express my deep appreciation to the book's photographer, my friend Douglas L. Mason-Fry. Each time we have worked together, I have valued his technical expertise, his creativity, his easygoing manner, and his gift of communicating genuinely with children. I believe these qualities have contributed to the beauty of his pictures, and I know they have resulted in a rewarding experience for me.

Introduction

I don't know if there will ever be peace on earth. I don't know if fighting is an inborn or a learned behavior. I do know that I have to behave in a way that assumes I can make a difference, because I am a teacher.

Many poems, songs, and sermons tell us that peace must come from within each of us before it can touch all of us. We pass this message on to our children, but we know that unless we model the skills of peacemaking and conflict resolution, our words are empty.

This book is a collection of photographs of children modeling these skills. Other children, and the adults who care about them, can read the words and discuss their meanings. They can dramatize the situations portrayed in these pictures. They can write poems and stories about the events that preceded or followed the moments captured in the book, or about what would have happened if the children in the book had not "made peace." And they can develop peacemaking strategies of their own.

Learning any skill takes practice, and peacemaking is a skill. I hope this book provides an opportunity for learning and practice. I hope it will make you smile.

And I hope someday there will be peace on earth.

How do you make peace?

Be happy

Make friends

Work together

Play together

Learn together

Talk about your feelings

Say you're sorry and shake hands

Help each other

Teach each other

19

Love each other

Listen

Count to 10 before you speak

Try to imagine how other people feel

Accept other points of view

Appreciate differences

Practice solving problems

Plan

Talk

Put your heads together

Stop and think

Look at it another way

Keep trying

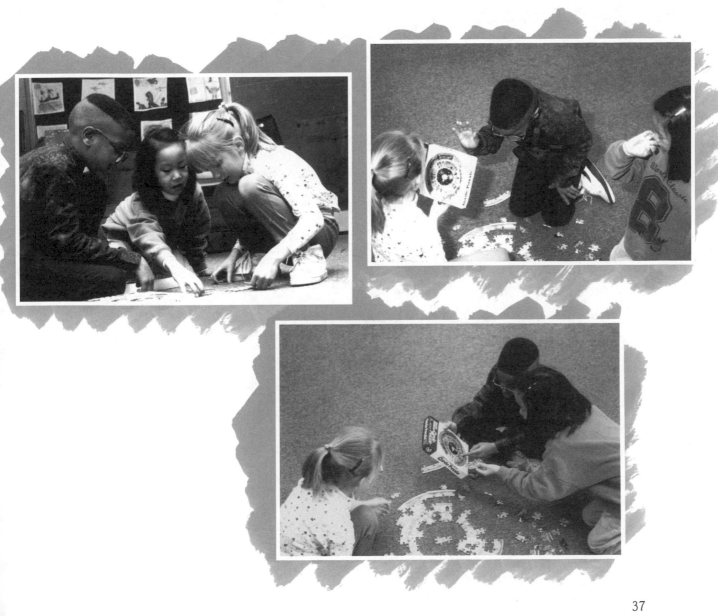

Be patient

Cooperate

Compromise

Forgive

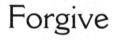

Make an agreement
(Sign a treaty)

Stop and smell the flowers

Share something special with someone

Smile

Make someone smile

When it's over,
         let it be over,
and move on

Follow the Golden Rule

Read

Relax

Remember

59

Sing

Dance

Dream

Imagine

Celebrate

How do *you* make peace?

About the author

Judy Lalli has been teaching for 25 years in Norristown, Pennsylvania. She holds B.S. and M.S. degrees from the University of Pennsylvania, and she has completed extensive postgraduate work as well. As an adjunct professor at Wilkes University and Allentown College, Judy teaches graduate education courses for teachers.

Make Someone Smile is Judy's third book. The first two, also photographed by Douglas L. Mason-Fry, are *At Least I'm Getting Better*, a blend of poems and photographs dealing with children's self-esteem and relationships, and *Feelings Alphabet*, a celebration of 26 emotions portrayed through photographs and word graphics.

Other Great Books from Free Spirit

I'm Like You, You're Like Me
A Child's Book About Understanding and Celebrating Each Other
by Cindy Gainer
"You and I are alike in many ways. We may be the same age or live on the same street.... We are different from each other, too." Simple words and lush illustrations draw children into this gentle story of discovery, acceptance, and affirmation. For ages 3–8. *$12.95; 48 pp.; softcover; color illus.; 11¼" x 9"*

Leader's Guide
For preschool through grade 3.
$16.95; 80 pp.; softcover; illus., 8½" x 11"

We Can Get Along
A Child's Book of Choices
by Lauren Murphy Payne, M.S.W., illustrated by Claudia Rohling, M.S.W.
Simple words and inviting illustrations teach children how to get along with others and resolve conflicts peacefully. For ages 3–8. *$9.95; 36 pp.; softcover; color illus.; 7⅝" x 9¼"*

Leader's Guide
For preschool through grade 3.
$14.95; 64 pp.; softcover; illus., 8½" x 11"

Just Because I Am
A Child's Book of Affirmation
by Lauren Murphy Payne, M.S.W., illustrated by Claudia Rohling, M.S.W.
Warm, simple words and enchanting full-color illustrations strengthen and support children's self-esteem. Ideal for early elementary, preschool, day care, and the home. For ages 3–8.
$9.95; 32 pp.; softcover; color illus.; 7⅝" x 9¼"

Leader's Guide
For preschool through grade 3.
$14.95; 56 pp.; softcover; illus., 8½" x 11"

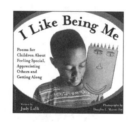

I Like Being Me
Poems for Children About Feeling Special, Appreciating Others, and Getting Along
by Judy Lalli, M.S., photographs by Douglas L. Mason-Fry
Rhyming poems and black and white photographs explore issues important to young children—being kind, solving problems, and more. For ages 3–8. *$9.95; 64 pp.; softcover; B&W photos; 8¼" x 7¼"*

To place an order or to request a free catalog of SELF-HELP FOR KIDS® and SELF-HELP FOR TEENS® materials, please write, call, email, or visit our Web site:

Free Spirit Publishing Inc.
217 Fifth Avenue North • Suite 200 • Minneapolis, MN 55401-1299
toll-free 800.735.7323 • local 612.338.2068 • fax 612.337.5050
help4kids@freespirit.com • www.freespirit.com